C

And I'm Hungry

(a camping cookbook & journal for motorcyclists – yes some of us do need one!)

Richard Mawson

One Motorbike, One Tent & I'm hungry

Richard Mawson has asserted his right to be identified as the author of this work in accordance with the Copyright, Designs and Patents act 1988

Although every effort has been made to trace the present copyright holders, we apologise in advance for any unintentional omission or neglect and will be happy to insert acknowledgements in any subsequent edition of this publication

First Edition 2012

Photographs

Front Cover © Richard Mawson
Back Cover © David Carson

© 2012 Richard Mawson. All rights reserved.
ISBN 978-1-300-40697-6

One Motorbike, One Tent & I'm hungry

Contents

Background 5

Kit Options 8

My Kit 9

Simple Guide To The Rest Of The Book 12

Breakfast..15
   Breakfast All Wrapped Up 16
   Fried Breakfast Sarni 19
   Bacon Butty For Two 21
   Omelette In A Bag 24
   Brunch In A Pan 27
   Your Ideas 29

Main Meals 35
   Pitta Bread and Houmous 36
   M's Spicy Sausage Stew............................38
   Chicken and Veg Hot Pot...........................40
   Chicken in Spicy Tomato Sauce with Rice 42
   Summer Veg Tagine..................................45
   Pork Chops with Savoy Cabbage Mash ..47
   Mixed Mushroom Frittata...........................50
   Spanish Chicken 53
   Bacon, Red Onion and Blue Cheese Pasta 56
   One Pot Moroccan Lamb With Eggs 58
   Campfire Supper 61
   M's Simple Hash..64
   Chicken Casserole 66
   Tabloid Trout 68

Sausage & Mash 71
Sausages with Apples and Cider 74
Bacon Stroganoff 77
Antipasto Platter 80
Mexican Bacon Tortillas 82
Sausage & Pepper Cassoulet 85
Poached Egg Salad with Parma Ham 87
Corned Beef and Egg Hash 90
Halloumi and Grape Salad 93
Turkish Salad 96
Bacon And Mushroom Pasta 99
One Pan Summer Eggs 101
Your Notes 103

Desserts 114

Acknowledgements 116

Background

First off, I'm not a chef or cook, nor do I know the nutritional value of any of these cooking ideas – I'm a biker who travels, camps and likes cooking simple rustic food.

So why write a book of recipes aimed at bikers?

Mmm, an interesting question, but over many years of travelling and camping and seeing what other people cooked at the end of the day I thought it was time to help more people away from 'boil in the bag' dehydrated pouches and chilli out of a tin/pouch. (But don't get me wrong, there is a place for good quality pouches, as I always have a pouch of 'Look what we found' chilli in my panniers as a just in case)

Also I recently had bought for me a 'Camping Cookbook' (I think written by someone who basically took their whole kitchen and oven with them) which had me smiling when I got to pages that said….. 'and simmer for 2 hours' or 'Pot Roast Pork Shoulder with Anchovies and Fennel – cooking time 3 hours'

Now in my head camp cooking should

- a) be easy
- b) not take longer than 30 to 45 mins from start to eating
- c) not need the kitchen store cupboard with you to cook it.

But if it's raining when you reach your destination, then it's not always a pleasing thought to have to get everything out and start to cook. So a bimble into the local village to find a pub or café works very nicely thank you.

Sometimes you just really can't be bothered to cook – and I've had some really nice meals in some of the places I've been. This also gets you interacting with locals (especially if you are abroad)

I know some adventure bikers like to think of themselves as explorers forging off into the unknown, riding hard and living off the land, however none of the recipes in this book require you to snare and skin a rabbit or stand for hours on a river bank trying to catch a fish (although you can if you want – I'm not stopping you!). They are just alternatives to popping a bag into boiling water and then using the same, now plastic flavoured water, to make coffee.

Some of the recipes use herbs and spices which can be a pain to carry with you (if you carried every herb and spice). If you don't have the right herb or spice, then try with what you have, or even without and see what it tastes like.

All the ingredients in the recipes can be easily found in any village shop, so you can shop after pitching the tent or shop on your way in.

Nearly all the recipes can be cooked on a two person stove (a couple need a larger pot). Some will need to be scaled down if you are solo riding/camping. And a few are best done in the hot embers of a fire

Don't forget, there are always ways round not being able to carry fresh food. A tin of potatoes is fine and cooks quicker than boiling a pan of fresh for mash for example, so think laterally sometimes.

Kit Options

Cookers

There is so much kit out there these days to choose from that a lot is down to personal choice. There is no need to buy the most expensive of everything (just because the sales man says so) – just grow into what's best for you.

For many years I just had a simple solid fuel burner as it was all I could afford and worked for me at that time. It was great if you wanted a totally uncontrollable fire and did cook basic food. At the other end of the scale a multi fuel burner is great as you will always have a supply of fuel from the bike if you run out of cooking fuel.

One thing is for sure – everyone will tell you that theirs is the best!

BBQs

I have to admit I've only bought disposable BBQ's once I'd got to a destination that I was staying at for some time. But a friend of mine carries a small collapsible BBQ which packs up nice and small which I think is fantastic. We made good use of it on a recent trip to the Dolomites to lift spirits after 11 days of constant rain sitting under a tarp cooking and watching the fire. Food is made for BBQ's with that smokey flavour and warmth.

My Kit

Cooker

I use a Trangia cookset as my main setup with the additional gas adaptor. This then gives me gas or meths as ignition (gas has the advantage of being more controllable). On longer trips, I also carry a simple gas burner that fits straight on top of the gas canister.

I like the Trangia format as everything fits into itself and you have everything you need in one item. I think mine is the 27-4UL model number, 1/2 person size with a non stick fry pan, two pans, kettle and burner. When it's all packed up, I've added a box of matches, a small 35mm film canister of washing up liquid and a washing sponge into the kettle.

Prep

Chopping Board

Mine is a simple plastic one made by cutting down a larger kitchen board so it would fit nicely in my pannier, but at the same time not be bigger than required.

Knives

1 basic cooks knife in a sheath
1 Gerber multi tool with a serrated edged blade

Other bits n' bobs

- A small non stick spatula
- Spork
- Olive oil in a small plastic squirt bottle (the type you get from Boots or the Pound shop in travel kits)
- Spice mix/mixed herbs in a small plastic bottle
- Self seal sandwich bags – useful for all sorts of stuff when on the bike
- Baco Cook in Bags
- Kitchen roll
- Sanitising hand gel – about 70p for 50ml from Aldi (no need to go to a camping shop and pay £2.99)
- 10l Water bladder – saves lots of trips to the tap

And I think that's about all the kit I carry for cooking. Yes I know some will say it's not enough and some will say it's far too much, but it works for me and that's the point I'm making – use what works for you, but remember you are on a motorbike and it all has to be light and fit somewhere.

Cut out a circle the size of your frying pan from a cheap kitchen chopping board. Then when your cook set is all packed up you really will have an all in one solution

Whatever happens, always remember a corkscrew and a bottle opener!

Simple Guide To The Rest Of The Book

I've kept things as simple as possible, that's probably cos I need recipes to be as simple as possible!

Anyway at the top of every recipe is a little box

M's Spicy Sausage Stew

Serves 2/3	Pots 1
Cooking level *	Washing up level **

Its not tricky to work it all out…..

Serves – A lot of this is down to how hungry you are, so it's a very rough guide.

Pots – This is always an important one for me cos I hate washing the pots up. (does not include plates and the like)

Cooking Level - * very easy, up to ***** well hard and not in this book!

Washing up level - * one easy pan to clean up to ***** a Sunday roast

Notes - To make the book more into a journal, after each cooking idea is a page for your notes. I have to admit, when I'm on a bike trip I like to keep a bit of a log of who, what, where, when, weather and the like. It only takes a few minutes of the day, but means I've got something to look back on to jog the old brain in years to come. Or if I changed a recipe I can write it down for next time.

Ive tried to keep exact measurements down to the basics because who carries a set of scales with them on a bike? Thinking about it, who carries scales at all!

TSP – Teaspoon

TBSP – Tablespoon

¼ Pint of water = about half an empty 400g tomato tin.

Herbs & Spices – Try to at least carry a small plastic bottle of mixed herbs as an 'it's not right, but it will do' solution. If you don't have any with you, then try without and see what it tastes like.

All the ingredients in the recipes can be easily found in any village shop, so you can buy after pitching the tent or buy on your way in.

That's about it really, so have a great ride, park up at the end of the day, find a local shop to buy some ingredients and have fun cooking a great meal and don't forget to open a beer or few (or wine if you are a posh biker!)

Breakfast

You wouldn't set out on the bike without enough fuel to get you to the next filling station, and the same is true for you! On a bike you need to stay alert and 'with it', and overnight the body slows down, so you need to wake it up again and a good breakfast does just that.

I'll admit that sometimes I just have a coffee and set off looking for a café or bakery on route – you don't have to cook all the time.

Breakfast All Wrapped Up

Serves 2	Pots 2
Cooking level *	Washing up level *

This is a cracking way to start a great day on the bike – sat outside your tent with a breakfast wrap in your hand.

Pack of Tortilla Wraps

Chutney

4 Eggs

4 Rashers of Bacon

4 Sausages

4 Slices of Black Pudding

Mushrooms

2 Big Toms

---

1. Hard boil the eggs, cool, peel and roughly chop
2. Chop bacon, sausages, black pud and mushrooms and fry until cooked
3. Spread chutney onto tortillas
4. Fill with egg and fry-up mix
5. Wrap it all up and enjoy with a nice coffee

No fridge* – use tinned baked beans and sausage, tinned mushrooms and tinned bacon grill.

*No fridge is easier than saying – no way of keeping fresh stuff cool all the time. It would have to be a big bike to have an integrated fridge. Mmmm perhaps Honda could look into that for the next GoldWing option.

Notes:

When/Where/Who/Weather/Recipe Notes

_____
_____
_____
_____
_____
_____
_____
_____
_____
_____
_____
_____
_____
_____
_____
_____
_____
_____

Fried Breakfast Sarni

| Serves 2 | Pots 1 |
| Cooking level * | Washing up level * |

An interesting twist on a breakfast butty – It's not a butty

---
2 Slices of Thick White Bread

2 Eggs

1 Tomato (sliced)

3 Rashers of Bacon (chopped)

Mushrooms (chopped)

---

1. Cut a decent size hole in the centre of each slice of bread
2. Fry the circles both sides until brown and set aside
3. Fry the mushrooms, tomato and bacon until cooked and set aside
4. Fry one side of the bread until brown, turn over and crack an egg into the hole. Fry until cooked
5. Spoon mushroom, tomato and bacon mix onto the cut out rounds and serve with the fried bread and egg

Notes:

When/Where/Who/Weather/Recipe Notes

_____

_____

_____

_____

_____

_____

_____

_____

_____

_____

_____

_____

_____

_____

_____

_____

_____

Bacon Butty For Two

Serves 2	Pots 1
Cooking level *	Washing up level **

A big sarni for a big appetite

4 Rashers of Back Bacon
3 Large Thick Slices of White Bread (best from unsliced loaf)
1 TSP Olive Oil
1 Tomato (thick sliced)
1 Large Mushroom (thick sliced)
2 Eggs (lightly beaten)
1 Green Chilli (deseeded and fine chopped)
Mayonnaise
1 TBSP Coriander (chopped)
1 TBSP Parsley (chopped)

1. Dry fry bacon for 3 – 4 mins until crispy. Remove and set aside
2. Heat the oil in the pan and cook the toms and mushroom slices until lightly cooked. Remove and set aside
3. Into the pan add the beaten egg chilli and herbs mix. Allow the mix to set, then turn over and brown the other side.

4. Construct the butty:
    a. On first bread slice place 2 rashers of bacon, the tomato and mushroom slices, then cover with the second bread slice
    b. Spread the top with mayonnaise, then the omelette and 2 rashers of bacon. Cover with the third slice of bread
5. Cut in half and enjoy

Top Tip

To save on washing up – break the eggs into a sandwich bag and 'squish' to beat them up

Notes:

When/Where/Who/Weather/Recipe Notes

_____

_____

_____

_____

_____

_____

_____

_____

_____

_____

_____

_____

_____

_____

_____

Omelette In A Bag

Serves 1	Pots 1
Cooking level *	Washing up level *

A great easy way to have a yummy omelette without the need for scraping out the frying pan

---
1 Baco Cook In Bag or Ziplock Bag (per omelette)

2 Eggs (large) (per omelette)

Filling (ideas – onion, ham, cheese, peppers, pre-cooked bacon or sausage, tomato – if you can think of it, then put it in (meat must be pre-cooked))

---

1. Fill a pan with water and bring to boil
2. Meanwhile, prepare the fillings of your choice
3. Crack 2 eggs into bag and shake or 'squidge' to combine. Then add any fillings
4. Remove as much air out of the bag as possible
5. Place the bag into the boiling water for 13 mins

6. Open the bag and serve – omelette with no fuss or mess

Notes:

When/Where/Who/Weather/Recipe Notes

_____

_____

_____

_____

_____

_____

_____

_____

_____

_____

_____

_____

_____

_____

_____

_____

_____

_____

Brunch In A Pan

Serves 2	Pots 1
Cooking level *	Washing up level *

Simple full English in a pan

---
1 TBSP Olive Oil

Handful or two of Mushrooms (halved)

2 or 3 Rashers of Back Bacon

200g Pack of Cherry Tomatoes (halved)

2 Eggs

Crusty Bread

---

1. Fry the bacon until nice and crisp.
2. Add the mushrooms and cook for about 5 mins until soft.
3. Add the tomatoes, then cook for a few mins more. Stir in a little seasoning
4. Then make two gaps in the mix and crack in the eggs. Cover the pan with a lid or a sheet of foil, then cook for 2-3 mins until the eggs are done to your liking.
5. Serve up with the bread

Notes:

When/Where/Who/Weather/Recipe Notes

_____

_____

_____

_____

_____

_____

_____

_____

_____

_____

_____

_____

_____

_____

_____

_____

Your Ideas

Right then, there are some of my ideas for breakfasts.

Over the next few pages are some blanks so now you have no excuse for forgetting how you made that great breakfast that time!

Title:

Serves	Pots
Cooking level	Washing up level

_____
_____
_____
_____
_____
_____
_____
_____
_____
_____
_____
_____
_____
_____
_____
_____
_____

Title:

Serves	Pots
Cooking level	Washing up level

_____

_____

_____

_____

_____

_____

_____

_____

_____

_____

_____

_____

_____

One Motorbike, One Tent & I'm hungry

Title:

Serves	Pots
Cooking level	Washing up level

_____

_____

_____

_____

_____

_____

_____

_____

_____

_____

_____

_____

_____

_____

_____

_____

_____

Title:

Serves	Pots
Cooking level	Washing up level

_____

_____

_____

_____

_____

_____

_____

_____

_____

_____

_____

_____

_____

_____

Title:

Serves	Pots
Cooking level	Washing up level

Main Meals

This part is just going to be main meals as you could eat them at any time of the day. Two meals a day is right for me, so at lunch I tend to just have a snack of something and a coffee break when on the road. And if you are on the road with somewhere to be, stopping to get all the cooking stuff out might be a bit of a pain, so for lunch stop at a local store and just enjoy where you are.

Pitta Bread and Houmous

Serves 1	Pots 0
Cooking level *	Washing up level *

Can't be bothered to cook, but want a nibble

Packet of Pita Breads
Big Tub of Houmous
2 Carrots
Rocket leaves

1. Finely slice the carrots
2. Open bread down one long edge and spoon in some homous. Add carrots and leaves
3. Dip in and relax

Notes:

When/Where/Who/Weather/Recipe Notes

_____

_____

_____

_____

_____

_____

_____

_____

_____

_____

_____

_____

_____

_____

_____

M's Spicy Sausage Stew

Serves 2/3	Pots 1
Cooking level *	Washing up level **

The perfect stew that tastes as though it's been cooking for hours.

4/6 Good Quality Sausages
1 TBSP Olive Oil
1 Onion (sliced)
1 Can of Tesco Hot & Spicy Mixed Beans
1 Tin of Toms in Chilli Sauce
Tom Puree (a good slug)
Crusty Bread

4. Heat oil and fry the sausages for 4 to 5 mins until golden – Remove and set aside
5. Cook onions in same pan for 5 to 6 mins until soft. Add beans, toms and puree and bring to the boil.
6. Cut sausages into threes and return to the pan. Lower the heat and simmer for about 6 or 7 mins until sausages are fully cooked
7. Serve with crusty bread.

Notes:

When/Where/Who/Weather/Recipe Notes

___
___
___
___
___
___
___
___
___
___
___
___
___
___
___

Chicken and Veg Hot Pot

Serves 4	Pots 1
Cooking level *	Washing up level *

You need a big pot for this one, but it is easily scaled down for 1 or 2

---

4 Chicken Breasts (with skin on if you can find them)

2 Parsnip (chopped)

2 Carrots (chopped)

300ml Ready Made Gravy

Cabbage (chopped handful)

---

1. Heat pan, add chicken skin side down and fry until golden.
2. Turn over and add parsnips and carrots and cook for 7 to 8 mins
3. Pour over the gravy and cook gently for 10 mins. Stir in the cabbage, cover and cook for 5 mins
4. Serve up and smile

Notes:

When/Where/Who/Weather/Recipe Notes

_____

_____

_____

_____

_____

_____

_____

_____

_____

_____

_____

_____

_____

_____

_____

Chicken in Spicy Tomato Sauce with Rice

Serves 3	Pots 2
Cooking level **	Washing up level ***

If you fancy a twist on a chilli out of a can then this is the one for you

1 TBSP oil

4 Chicken Thighs or Breasts

1 Can Chopped Tomatoes in Chilli Sauce

1 Can of Chilli Beans

½ Onion

½ Courgette

Rice – Uncle Bens Express Rice

OR Normal Rice

1. Pour a little of the oil into a pan and brown the chicken on both sides.
2. Drain away any excess fat. Pour in can of toms and beans. Stir, cover and cook over a gentle heat for about 20 mins until chicken is cooked. Meanwhile, dice the onion and courgette.
3. Heat remaining oil in a pan, add the onion and courgette and cook till soft.

4. Add the rice and cook for a minute.
5. Add 30ml of water, bring to the boil, then simmer for 3 mins. Serve the rice with the chicken and sauce.

Note:

If using normal rice at #4 add 200g long grain rice. Cook for 1 min, pour 550ml of water, stir and cook at a simmer for 15 to 20 min.

Notes:

When/Where/Who/Weather/Recipe Notes

Summer Veg Tagine

Serves 2	Pots 2
Cooking level *	Washing up level **

Make this for a taste of Morocco at your camp

---

1 Pack 100g Ainsley Harriott Spice Sensation Cous Cous (or similar)

2 Tomatoes

½ Large Red Chilli

½ Courgette

½ Red Pepper

4 Ready To Eat Dried Apricots

½ TBSP Coriander

---

1. Make cous cous as per the packet
2. Dice up the tomatoes. Deseed and dice the chilli. Put both in pan, cover and cook gently until soft.
3. Meanwhile, cut courgette into batons, slice the pepper, halve the apricots.
4. Add to the toms and cook on a high heat for a few mins stirring till cooked.
5. Stir veg into cous cous and sprinkle with coriander

Works well with some BBQ lamb or chicken.

Notes:

When/Where/Who/Weather/Recipe Notes

_____

_____

_____

_____

_____

_____

_____

_____

_____

_____

_____

Pork Chops with Savoy Cabbage Mash

Serves 4	Pots 2
Cooking level ***	Washing up level ***

The timing can be a pain on this one, but the end result is worth it

---

4 or 5 Large Potatoes (chopped into chunks)

½ Small Savoy Cabbage (the curly one) (sliced)

50g Butter (a good big spoon full)

4 Nice Pork Chops

200g Ready Made Onion Gravy

Water

---

1. Put potatoes in a large pan of water. Cover, bring to the boil and simmer for 10 mins. After 5 mins add the cabbage to the pan

2. When cooked, drain, mash up and keep warm

3. Meanwhile heat a fry pan or BBQ. Rub butter onto each chop. Fry/BBQ chops for 4 to 5 mins each side until cooked. Set aside

4. Add gravy to pan, bring to the boil and simmer for a minute or two
5. Spoon mash onto plates, add the chops and pour over the gravy.

Notes:

When/Where/Who/Weather/Recipe Notes

_____

_____

_____

_____

_____

_____

_____

_____

_____

_____

_____

_____

_____

_____

_____

Mixed Mushroom Frittata

Serves 2 hungry bikers	Pots 1
Cooking level **	Washing up level **

A posh name for a big mushroom omelette

---
1 TBSP olive oil

300g Mixed Mushrooms (sliced)

½ Lemon (zest and juice)

6 Eggs

50g Watercress (chopped)

2 TBSP Fresh Thyme

Crusty Bread

Salad Bag

---

1. Heat oil in fry pan. Add mushrooms and thyme and stir fry for 5 mins until starting to soften. Stir in the lemon juice and zest. Bubble for a minute, then lower the heat down.
2. Break the eggs into a self seal sandwich bag, and mix together. Add the watercress and mix, and then pour into the pan. Cook for 7 to 8 mins until cooked.

3. Flip and cook until set through
4. Serve with crusty bread and a crispy salad.

Top Tip

To flip the omelette slide it out of the pan onto a plate, then tip it back into the pan the other way up. No heroics required here.

If you don't have any sandwich bags then another pot is required for mixing the eggs and watercress

Notes:

When/Where/Who/Weather/Recipe Notes

Spanish Chicken

Serves 2 real hungry bikers or 3 normal bikers	Pots 1
Cooking level *	Washing up level **

Why reinvent the wheel, when you can customise something thats nearly perfect. This is a dish I make time and time again – its just spot on, and so simple. Great with just loads of crusty bread

---

1 Packet Swartz Spanish Chicken Mix!!!

1 TBSP Olive Oil

450g Chicken Breast (cut into strips)

OR A Big Packet of Ready Cooked Chicken Breast Pieces

5 Rashers of Smoked Bacon (sliced)

1 Yellow Pepper (chopped)

Tom Puree (a couple of nice big slugs)

¼ Pint of Water (see notes)

1 400g Tin of Chopped Tomatoes

Chorizo (as much as you fancy) (sliced)

Uncle Bens Express Rice **OR** Crusty Bread

---

1. Heat oil and fry chicken (if using fresh), bacon and chorizo for about 8 mins.

2. Throw in pepper and chicken (if using ready cooked) and sprinkle in the mix. Cook for 1 min

3. Add tomato puree, toms and water. Simmer for 15 mins till the sauce has thickened.

4. Serve with the rice (cook as per packet – only about 3 mins) OR nice crusty bread.

¼ pint of water – about half the empty tomato tin

Notes:

When/Where/Who/Weather/Recipe Notes

_____

_____

_____

_____

_____

_____

_____

_____

_____

_____

_____

_____

_____

_____

_____

_____

Bacon, Red Onion and Blue Cheese Pasta

Serves 2	Pots 2
Cooking level *	Washing up level **

Simple and satisfying pasta dish

> 200g Pasta
>
> 1 TBSP Oil
>
> 1 Red Onion (peeled & cut into wedges – tip to root)
>
> 4 or 5 Rashers of Bacon (cut into strips)
>
> 75g Soft Blue Cheese (dolcelatte or similar)
>
> Chives (handful chopped)
>
> Water

1. Bring pan of water to the boil and cook pasta as per the pack
2. Heat oil in fry pan until hot and fry onions for about 5 mins. Add the bacon and fry for a few mins more until cooked.
3. Drain pasta (when cooked) and add to bacon and onion along with cubes of the cheese. Turn heat right down and allow the cheese to melt a little

4. Season and scatter over the chives to serve

Notes:

When/Where/Who/Weather/Recipe Notes

_____
_____
_____
_____
_____
_____
_____
_____
_____
_____
_____
_____

One Pot Moroccan Lamb With Eggs

Serves 4 but easy to scale down to 1 or 2	Pots 1
Cooking level ***	Washing up level **

Can be a tricky one this, but it's worth it.

Pack of Ready Made Lamb Meatballs

1 Garlic Clove (finely sliced)

1 TBSP Ginger (grated)

1 onion (chopped)

1 Big TSP Moroccan Spice Mix

400g Tin Chopped Tomatoes

4 Eggs

Handful of Mint Leaves

Water

Crusty Bread or Cous Cous to serve

---

1. Heat oil in large deep fry pan. Add meatballs and cook for 3 mins on each side until golden all over. Remove any excess fat. Add onion, garlic and ginger to pan and cook for a few mins until soft.

2. Stir in Moroccan spice mix, then pour over the toms and ½ a tin of water.

Bring to the boil, then simmer for 20 mins.

3. Make four hollows into the mix and crack an egg into each one. Cover and leave eggs to poach for 5 mins.
4. Scatter over the mint leaves and serve with crusty bread of cous cous.

Note

Moroccan Spice mix can be bought at any supermarket and really adds a taste of North Africa to any dish.

I don't carry this all the time (usually have mixed herbs), I only carry this when I'm thinking of making it.

Notes:

When/Where/Who/Weather/Recipe Notes

Campfire Supper

Serves 2	Pots 1
Cooking level **	Washing up level *

A bit of a blokey type fire is needed for this, but there is nothing better than a baked potato cooked in a fire.

2 to 3 Large Baking Potatoes
2 to 3 Eggs
Cheese (grated)
1 Tin Baked Beans
2 Bananas
Packet of Chocolate Buttons
Foil
Oh and a fire

1. Cut the top third off each potato and save.
2. Cut out a hollow in the larger section of each potato, add grated cheese, then break an egg into the hole. Replace lid and seal with a couple of small sticks
3. Double wrap in foil and place in the embers of a hot fire for 45 mins to 1hour until cooked

4. Serve with baked beans

Part Two

1. Peal the bananas along one side and push chocolate buttons into the flesh.
2. Reseal the skin, wrap with foil and bake in the fire embers for 10(ish) mins
3. Serve out of the foil

Notes:

When/Where/Who/Weather/Recipe Notes

_____
_____
_____
_____
_____
_____
_____
_____
_____
_____
_____
_____
_____
_____
_____
_____
_____

M's Simple Hash

Serves 1 to 2	Pots 1
Cooking level *	Washing up level *

Simple, simple, simple but tastes great and is filling

1 Large Tin Big Soup (of your choice)
1 Medium Size Tin of Corned Beef (cubed)
Crusty Bread

1. Warm soup and then add corned beef cubes.
2. Stir to break down the beef
3. Serve with crusty bread

What a great way to end the day with something that looks and tastes so nice – hard to beat it

Notes:

When/Where/Who/Weather/Recipe Notes

_____

_____

_____

_____

_____

_____

_____

_____

_____

_____

_____

_____

_____

_____

_____

_____

Chicken Casserole

Serves 2	Pots 1
Cooking level *	Washing up level *

A real filler of a meal

---

1 Large Packet of Ready Cooked Chicken Pieces

1 Can Condensed Chicken Soup

1 Tin of Peas

1 Small Red Pepper (chopped)

1 Large Cup of Rice

1 Chicken or Veg Stock Cube

Water

Crusty Fresh Bread

---

1. Mix the chicken, peas, pepper, rice into the soup
2. Add the stock cube and cook gently for 20 min until the rice is tender
3. Add a little water as required
4. Serve with crusty bread

Notes:

When/Where/Who/Weather/Recipe Notes

_____

_____

_____

_____

_____

_____

_____

_____

_____

_____

_____

_____

_____

_____

_____

_____

Tabloid Trout

Serves 1/2	Pots 1
Cooking level **	Washing up level *

If its fish you like then is a great way to cook it when out on the road – over a fire

---
1 Tabloid Newspaper (of your choice)

1 or 2 Trout (prepared)

Rosemary

Lemon

1 Pack of Cous Cous

Cherry Tomatoes

Green Salad Bag

Butter

Water

---

1. Soak the newspaper in water for about 5 mins. Open out and put the fish in the centre. Add a little rosemary, a knob of butter and some lemon juice inside the fish.
2. Wrap newspaper around the fish to form a parcel and place over fire or BBQ for about 30 mins.

3. Turn after 15 mins and keep the paper wet so that the fish steams.
4. Meanwhile make up the cous cous
5. Open the wine and salad bag and serve

Note:

Its not always easy to keep butter when you are on a bike, but if staying in the same spot for a few days it might be worth it.

Notes:

When/Where/Who/Weather/Recipe Notes

Sausage & Mash

Serves 2	Pots 1 (2 if having beans)
Cooking level *	Washing up level **

A spicy one pot twist to sausage and mash – no mash

---
4 Sausages

Cup of Rice

1 Large Red Onion (chopped)

1 Tin Chopped Tomatoes

1 Celery Stick (chopped)

1 Veg Stock Cube

1 Tin of Baked Beans (the curry type)

Crusty Bread

Water

---

1. Brown the sausages in a pan, then add the onion, rice and celery and cook for a few mins stirring.
2. Add the toms, stock cube, and a little water. Cover and cook on a low heat for about 20mins.
3. Serve up with the baked beans and bread

One Motorbike, One Tent & I'm hungry

Notes:

When/Where/Who/Weather/Recipe Notes

_____

_____

_____

_____

_____

_____

_____

_____

_____

_____

_____

_____

_____

_____

_____

Sausages with Apples and Cider

Serves 2	Pots 2
Cooking level **	Washing up level **

Posh sausage and mash. Not everyone's idea of camp food but why not try something a bit different

> 6 Good Sausages
>
> 75g Butter (a big spoon full)
>
> 3 Big Dessert Apples
>
> 150ml Dry Cider
>
> 100ml Double Cream
>
> 6 Juniper Berries (crushed) (works ok without)
>
> 2 Big Potatoes for mash

1. Cut potatoes into cubes and put in a pan to boil
2. Over a low heat fry the sausages in half the butter
3. Quarter and core the apples, then slice into segments. Fry them in the remaining butter till they have softened a little. Lift apples out and set aside.
4. Add the cider to the pan with the juniper berries. Turn the heat up and let the

cider bubble down to half. Pour in the cream and leave to simmer for a few mins.

5. Place the sausages onto the apples and pour the sauce over both.
6. Mash the potatoes and serve

Notes:

When/Where/Who/Weather/Recipe Notes

_____

_____

_____

_____

_____

_____

_____

_____

_____

_____

_____

_____

_____

_____

_____

Bacon Stroganoff

Serves 2/3	Pots 2
Cooking level **	Washing up level **

This one has a nice creamy sauce. The wine really adds to the taste

---

8 Rashers of Back Bacon

½ TBSP Veg Oil

Knob of Butter

1 Small Onion (chopped)

1 TSP Paprika

170g Mushrooms (halved – chestnut it poss)

Big glass of Dry White Wine

Small carton Sour Cream

Uncle Bens Express Rice

---

1. Fry the bacon for about 4 mins until crispy. Remove and set aside.
2. Add oil and butter to the pan and heat gently. Stir in onion and cook for 5 mins until soft
3. Sprinkle over the paprika and mushrooms and cook for another 3 to 4 mins. Turn up the heat, add the wine and bubble until reduced by half.

4. Add the sour cream and stir through. Return bacon to pan and cook over a low heat until warmed through.
5. Serve with Rice

Notes:

When/Where/Who/Weather/Recipe Notes

Antipasto Platter

Serves as required	Pots 0
Cooking level *	Washing up level *

A real Italian favourite (and mine). Antipasto basically means 'before the meal', but I can easily have this as a meal. Just more bread, meat and cheese. Perfect for a sunny evening in Italy after a day on the bike

Meats : Parma Ham – Dry Cured Italian Ham
　　　　Napoli Salami
　　　　Spianata Calabrese
Cheese: Parmigiano Reggiano
　　　　Gorgonzola Ermorinato
　　　　Dolcelatte
　　　　Any local Cheese
Bread:　Ciabatta
Olives　Try and get some in a resealable pouch
Olive Oil for Dipping

1. Lay it all out and tuck in
2. The bread is great dipped in oil

How easy does it get – and not a tin of beans in sight!

Notes:

When/Where/Who/Weather/Recipe Notes

Mexican Bacon Tortillas

Serves 1/2	Pots 2
Cooking level *	Washing up level *

Mexico in a tortilla

---
3 Rashers of Back Bacon

1 TSP Oil

½ Onion (chopped)

1 200g Tin Chopped Tomatoes

1 Garlic Clove (crushed)

1 Tin Tesco Hot & spicy Mixed Beans

2 Large Tortillas

Grated Cheese

---

1. Cut bacon into chunks and fry for 4 mins until cooked. Remove from pan, and set aside
2. Add oil to pan and fry onions for 5 mins
3. Add the toms, garlic and beans, and simmer for about 10 to 15 mins. Return bacon back to the pan and warm through.
4. Warm the tortillas (either in another fry pan or metal plate, or be manly and hold them over the flame)

5. Spread equal amounts of the filling over each one. Cover with loads of grated cheese.

6. Roll and enjoy

Top Tip

Not wanting to tell you stuff you already know, but I find the best way to roll these is to put the filling in the centre towards the top. Then fold the bottom up and then the sides in. That way nothing falls out the bottom – and we really don't want that!

Notes:

When/Where/Who/Weather/Recipe Notes

Sausage & Pepper Cassoulet

Serves 2	Pots 1
Cooking level *	Washing up level *

Sausage and beans in a tomato sauce. Nice simple and yummy

225g Nice Thick Pork Sausages (about 4)

½ Onion (sliced)

½ Red Pepper (sliced)

Small Tin of Cannellini Beans (drained)

200g Tin of Chopped Tomatoes

---

1. Fry the sausages in a pan (not a frying pan) until browned. Add the onion and pepper along with the beans and tomatoes. (basically throw it all in the pan)
2. Bring to the boil, turn down the heat, cover and simmer for about 20mins until sausages are cooked through.

Notes:

When/Where/Who/Weather/Recipe Notes

Poached Egg Salad with Parma Ham

Serves 2	Pots 1
Cooking level *	Washing up level *

A salad with a twist. Cutting open the egg and letting the yolk run - perfect

---

Salad Bag of Mixed Leaves

Lettuce of Choice (shredded)

8 Plum Tomatoes (quartered)

4 Eggs

1 TBSP Olive Oil

2 TBSP Lemon Juice

1 Big TSP Dijon Mustard

8/10 Slices Parma Ham

Box of Bread Sticks

---

1. Mix together the salad bag and lettuce and tomatoes. Divide between the plates
2. Poach the eggs in gently simmering water for 2 to 4 mins until cooked to your liking. Meanwhile make the dressing by mixing together the oil, lemon juice and mustard.

3. Wrap a slice of ham around a bread stick. Place eggs on top of the salad.
4. Start by serving each with 2 breadsticks. Then more as needed.

Top Tip

Don't know how to poach an egg? Don't want to spend 20 mins cleaning the pan? Here's what to do:

1. Get some microwaveable clingfilm or a boil bag (clingfilm is better)
2. Get a cup
3. Push the cling film/bag into the cup, and crack the egg into the cling film
4. You should be able to tie the clingfilm around the top of the egg.
5. Drop egg into boiling water, and poach normally (2 mins for a soft egg, 4 mins for a firmer one), it'll taste great, and you wont have to spend ages scrubbing cooked on egg off the damn pan.

Notes:

When/Where/Who/Weather/Recipe Notes

Corned Beef and Egg Hash

Serves 1	Pots 1
Cooking level *	Washing up level **

A big pan of loveliness

½ TBSP Oil

Spoon Of Butter

½ Onion (chopped)

½ Small Green Pepper (diced)

Small Tin Of Potatoes (diced)

½ Tin Corned Beef

1 Egg

Tomato Ketchup (pinched from a café)

Sandwich Bag

---

1. Heat the oil and butter together in a frying pan and add the onion. Fry for about 5 mins

2. In the sandwich bag mix together the pepper, corned beef and potatoes. Add to the pan and mix gently. Press down lightly as you fry for about 4 mins until a golden brown crust has formed on the bottom.

3. Stir through to distribute the crust, and then fry again until the mix is well browned.
4. Make a well in the hash and crack an egg into it. Cover to poach the egg until the whites are just set.
5. Serve with tomato ketchup

Top Tip

Whenever you stop for a coffee always have a look for some packets of sauce, or salt and pepper

Notes:

When/Where/Who/Weather/Recipe Notes

Halloumi and Grape Salad

Serves 2 hungry bikers	Pots 1
Cooking level **	Washing up level *

Great for a sunny evening at camp – and even better with a dry white wine

---

Salad Bag of Mixed Leaves

Handful of Green Grapes

Handful of Black Grapes

250g Halloumi Cheese (sliced)

3 TBSP Olive Oil

For The Dressing

4 TBSP Olive Oil

Lemon (juiced)

½ TSP Sugar *

Salt & Pepper *

Sandwich Bag

---

1. To make the dressing, 'squidge' together the oil, lemon juice and sugar in the sandwich bag. Add salt and pepper to taste

2. Toss together the leaves with the grapes and put on a large serving plate.

3. Heat oil in frying pan. Add the cheese and fry briefly until it turns golden. Turn and cook the other side

4. Place cheese onto salad and pour over the dressing

Top Tip

The cheese is even better if cooked on a BBQ

*acquired from a café at a coffee stop during the day

Notes:

When/Where/Who/Weather/Recipe Notes

_____
_____
_____
_____
_____
_____
_____
_____
_____
_____
_____
_____
_____
_____
_____
_____
_____

Turkish Salad

Serves 2 hungry bikers	Pots 1
Cooking level *	Washing up level *

A salad with a bit of body. Lots of ingredients, but no cooking required

Salad Bag of Lettuce
1 Green Pepper
1 Red Pepper
1 Red Onion
½ Cucumber
4 Tomatoes
Block of Feta Cheese
Pouch of Black Olives
For The Dressing
3 TBSP Olive Oil
Lemon (juiced)
1 Garlic Clove (crushed)
Salt & Pepper *
2 Sandwich Bags
Fresh crusty bread

1. To make the dressing, 'squidge' together the oil, lemon juice and garlic in the sandwich bag. Add salt and pepper to taste
2. Cut the tomatoes and cucumber into small cubes. Finely chop the onion and tear up the lettuce leaves.
3. Put it all into a sandwich bag and mix lightly together
4. Place on a serving plate and pour dressing over.

Top Tip

*acquired from a café at a coffee stop during the day

Notes:

When/Where/Who/Weather/Recipe Notes

Bacon And Mushroom Pasta

Serves 2	Pots 1
Cooking level *	Washing up level **

Pasta was made for this dish

200g penne (or other tube shape) pasta
125g pack chestnut or button mushrooms
4 rashers streaky bacon
2 tbsp pesto (a jar of your choice)
100ml carton crème fraîche
handful basil leaves

1. Cook the pasta in boiling water in a large non-stick saucepan according to pack instructions. Meanwhile, slice the mushrooms and cut the bacon into bite-size pieces with a sharp knife.

2. Reserve a bit of the cooking water in a cup, then drain the pasta and set aside. Fry the bacon and mushrooms in the same pan until golden, about 5 mins. Keep the heat high so the mushrooms fry in the bacon fat, rather than sweat.

3. Tip the pasta and reserved water back into the pan and stir over the heat for 1 min. Take the pan off the heat, spoon in

the pesto and crème fraîche and most of the basil and stir to combine. Sprinkle with the remaining basil to serve.

One Pan Summer Eggs

Serves 2	Pots 1
Cooking level *	Washing up level **

A simple dish and ready in about 15 minutes

---

1 TBSP Olive Oil

400g Courgette (about 2) (chopped into small chunks)

200g Pack of Cherry Tomatoes

1 Garlic Clove

2 Eggs

Crusty Bread

---

1. Heat the oil in a non-stick frying pan, then add the courgettes. Fry for 5 mins, stirring every so often until they start to soften

2. Add the tomatoes and garlic, then cook for a few mins more. Stir in a little seasoning.

3. Then make two gaps in the mix and crack in the eggs. Cover the pan with a lid or a sheet of foil, then cook for 2-3 mins until the eggs are done to your liking, and serve with crusty bread.

Notes:

When/Where/Who/Weather/Recipe Notes

Your Notes

Right then, there are some of my ideas for main meals.

Again I've left some blanks so you can add in your own ideas and then the book really becomes yours.

Title:

Serves	Pots
Cooking level	Washing up level

Title:

Serves	Pots
Cooking level	Washing up level

_____

_____

_____

_____

_____

_____

_____

_____

_____

_____

_____

_____

_____

_____

_____

_____

_____

Title:

Serves	Pots
Cooking level	Washing up level

_____

_____

_____

_____

_____

_____

_____

_____

_____

_____

_____

_____

_____

_____

Title:

Serves	Pots
Cooking level	Washing up level

_____
_____
_____
_____
_____
_____
_____
_____
_____
_____
_____
_____
_____
_____
_____
_____

Title:

Serves	Pots
Cooking level	Washing up level

_____

_____

_____

_____

_____

_____

_____

_____

_____

_____

_____

_____

_____

_____

Title:

Serves	Pots
Cooking level	Washing up level

_____

_____

_____

_____

_____

_____

_____

_____

_____

_____

_____

_____

_____

_____

_____

_____

Title:

Serves	Pots
Cooking level	Washing up level

_____

_____

_____

_____

_____

_____

_____

_____

_____

_____

_____

_____

_____

_____

Title:

Serves	Pots
Cooking level	Washing up level

_____

_____

_____

_____

_____

_____

_____

_____

_____

_____

_____

_____

_____

_____

_____

_____

_____

One Motorbike, One Tent & I'm hungry

Title:

Serves	Pots
Cooking level	Washing up level

_____

_____

_____

_____

_____

_____

_____

_____

_____

_____

_____

_____

_____

_____

_____

Title:

Serves	Pots
Cooking level	Washing up level

_____

_____

_____

_____

_____

_____

_____

_____

_____

_____

_____

_____

_____

_____

_____

_____

Desserts

This section of the book is going to disappoint anyone who likes a nice sticky dessert.

I tend not to have desserts, so in a nut shell, I don't make them! But see **Campfire Supper** for bananas and chocolate cooked in a fire.

So, if you want a dessert bimble off to the shops and buy something gooey and sticky, or if you are like me, just open another beer, chill and enjoy the evening – even better with a fire.

One Motorbike, One Tent & I'm hungry

Acknowledgements

These recipes have been collected and adapted by myself over quite some time, so for most of them I have no idea now where they originated from.

The ones I do are credited here along with other acknowledgements:

- Spanish Chicken – adapted from a recipe by Swartz
- Mexican Bacon Tortillas – adapted from a recipe by Morrisons
- Sausages with Apples & Cider – Nigel Slater
- Corned Beef and Egg Hash – Jenni Fleetwood
- Halloumi and Grape Salad – Jenni Fleetwood
- 'Look what we found' - http://www.lookwhatwefound.co.uk

One Motorbike, One Tent & I'm hungry

Printed in Great Britain
by Amazon.co.uk, Ltd.,
Marston Gate.